The Louisiana Purchase

The Louisiana Purchase

Gloria G. Schlaepfer

Franklin Watts
A Division of Scholastic Inc.
New York • Toronto • London • Auckland • Sydney
Mexico City • New Delhi • Hong Kong
Danbury, Connecticut

This book is dedicated to all those students of history who want to learn more about the Louisiana Purchase.

Note to readers: Definitions for words in **bold** can be found in the Glossary at the back of this book.

Photographs © 2005: Art Resource, NY/C. Jean/Réunion des Musées Nationaux: 12; Corbis Images: 6, 14, 21, 23, 26, 43 (Bettmann), 38 (Jacques-Louis David/Archivo Iconografico, S.A.), 28 (Francisco Jose de Goya y Lucientes/Archivo Iconografico, S.A.), 41 (Francis G. Mayer), 32 (Gianni Dagli Orti), 16 (William Henry Powell/PoodlesRock), 13 (Alfred Russell/Bettmann), 48; Getty Images: 20 (H. Bridgman/Hulton Archive), 9, 22 (MPI/Hulton Archive); Library of Congress: 44; North Wind Picture Archives: 10, 18, 19, 30, 33, 34, 36, 40, 51, 52; PictureHistory.com/Allyn Cox: 2; The Art Archive/Picture Desk/Joseph Martin/Naval Museum: 24.

Cover map by Matt Kania/Map Hero, Inc.

The map on the cover shows the extend of the Louisiana Purchase.
The mural painting opposite the title page shows the signing of the Louisiana Purchase.

Library of Congress Cataloging-in-Publication Data

Schlaepfer, Gloria G.
  The Louisiana Purchase / Gloria G. Schlaepfer.
      p. cm. — (Watts library)
  Includes bibliographical references and index.
  ISBN 0-531-12300-6
 1. Louisiana Purchase—Juvenile literature. 2. United States—History—1801–1809—Juvenile literature.
 3. Napoleon I, Emperor of the French, 1769–1821—Relations with Americans—Juvenile literature.
 4. United States—Territorial expansion—Juvenile literature. I. Title. II. Series.
  E333.S35 2005
  973.4'6—dc22   2005001465

Contents

Charles Maurice de Talleyrand was the French prime minister who proposed selling the Louisiana territory to the United States.

Chapter One

The Greatest Land Deal

"Monsieur Ambassador, what would you give for the whole of Louisiana?" asked the French foreign minister, Charles Maurice de Talleyrand. The American ambassador, Robert Livingston, stood speechless. He had been instructed by President Thomas Jefferson to buy the port of New Orleans and, if possible, East Florida and West Florida from France.

All of Louisiana was beyond Livingston's wildest expectations. But there

Avoiding War

In October 1802, Spain's King Charles IV closed the port of New Orleans to American ships. Americans could no longer deposit, or store, their goods in the port's warehouses. Angry American citizens threatened to take the port by force. To avoid war, President Jefferson decided to try to buy the port.

it was! The dictator of France, Napoléon Bonaparte, had made the hasty decision to sell all the territory of Louisiana to the United States. Livingston asked Talleyrand for time to consider the offer and to await the arrival of James Monroe. As a special representative, Monroe was being sent to Paris to work with Livingston to **negotiate** a settlement with France. Jefferson's instructions to Monroe were to offer $10 million for New Orleans and East and West Florida, or $7 million for New Orleans alone.

Jefferson added, "Should a greater sum be made an **ultimatum** on the part of France, the President has made up his mind to go as far as 50 million of livres tournois [old French currency], rather than lose the main object" [New Orleans].

Monroe and Livingston recognized the French offer as a great opportunity. They had to reply quickly and could not wait for a letter of approval from the president to cross the Atlantic Ocean. Acting on their own, they negotiated with France and purchased the Louisiana territories for $15 million (60 million **francs**). The more than 800,000 square

THE LOUISIANA PURCHASE.
MESSRS. MONROE AND LIVINGSTONE COMPLETING NEGOTIATIONS WITH TALLYRAND, APRIL 30, 1803

miles (2.1 million square kilometers) of land west of the Mississippi River doubled the size of the young country. The greatest land deal in American history was a triumph for the United States. And it was achieved peacefully, without going to war.

Many Americans viewed the purchase as a **windfall.** Others were opposed to it. Some congressional representatives from the eastern states feared westward expansion and the admission of new states to the Union. They reasoned it might

Monroe (left), Livingston (center), and Talleyrand (right) complete negotiations for the Louisiana Purchase.

This map shows the United States in 1803, including the Louisiana Purchase.

shift political power away from the Atlantic states. Many other representatives denounced the purchase as unconstitutional, or illegal. They argued the Constitution had no provisions that gave the federal government the right to buy land from a foreign nation. Despite those concerns and objections, Congress ratified, or approved, the treaty on October 20, 1803.

Raising the Stars and Stripes

The United States gained possession of Louisiana on December 20, 1803, in New Orleans. William C. Claiborne, governor of the Mississippi Territory, and General James Wilkinson, governor of the District of Louisiana, represented the United States. In a formal ceremony, the French **prefect,** Pierre Clément de Laussat, presented Louisiana to the United States on behalf of France and Napoléon Bonaparte. The French flag, called the tricolor, then slid swiftly down the flagpole, and a cannon boomed. American soldiers lifted their **muskets** and fired into the air, a salute to the occasion.

As the Stars and Stripes rose to the top of the flagpole, the Americans shouted and waved their hats in celebration. In contrast, the Creoles—the French and Spanish townspeople of New Orleans—stood in stony silence. A few sobbed openly.

Laussat was visibly saddened, too. "What a magnificent New France we lost!" he exclaimed. His words expressed the feelings of many French people. The dream of a French empire in North America had been crushed. That evening, Laussat regained his composure and gave a dinner party for

Creoles

The word *Creole* describes the descendants of early French and Spanish settlers of Louisiana and their African slaves. Creole comes from the Spanish word *criollo,* meaning "white child born in the colonies." Creole food, such as spicy red beans and rice, is popular in many places in the United States.

450 guests. Champagne flowed, and dignitaries gave stirring tributes to the occasion.

Elastic Boundaries

The vast land of the Louisiana Territory lay between the Mississippi River and the Rocky Mountains, and stretched from Canada to the Gulf of Mexico. Yet the French were not certain of its boundaries. It took another fifteen years of war and negotiations to set the boundaries officially.

In an agreement with Great Britain in 1818, the 49th Parallel became the northern border of the territory. Likewise, in 1819, the Adams-Onís Treaty defined the southern border with the Spanish territory. The border would follow the Sabine, Arkansas, and Red rivers to the **Continental Divide.**

The changing of the flag ceremony at New Orleans in 1803

What Did It Mean?

The greatest land deal has been described as a stroke of luck for the young **republic.** Had the negotiations ended differently, the history and settlement of the United States might be quite unlike what we know today.

If France had not sold Louisiana, it would have continued to control the port of New Orleans, as well as com-

The ceremony of land transfer, officially making Louisiana part of the United States

merce on the Mississippi River. France might have tried to expand its holdings in North America by regaining Canada and forming a large French colony.

Spain and England surely would have tried to take control of parts of the continent. Spain, with settlements in the Southwest, including California, also had claims to land in southern Louisiana. England controlled Canada and its trading posts. England declared ownership of the land along the Pacific Coast, now called Washington and Oregon. It is possible that England would have tried to connect them to its lands in Canada. A struggle between the United States and the European powers over land would have resulted.

The history of the Louisiana Territory is a long one. It is a story about explorers, settlers, kings and their ministers, and American presidents. Wars, secret schemes and treaties, and control of a seaport affected the eventual outcome.

A Spanish galleon sails toward the Americas in search of riches.

Chapter Two

Exploration and Settlement

Within two decades after Columbus's 1492 landing in the West Indies, Spanish explorers and soldiers flocked to the Americas. At the time, Spain was the most powerful and wealthy nation in Europe. Its conquests in the Americas greatly expanded the Spanish empire, and the tons of gold and silver seized in the toppled lands increased the country's wealth.

English Pirates

English adventurers, such as Francis Drake, found riches in attacking and capturing Spanish galleons, or sailing ships, filled with gold and gems.

In the sixteenth century, Spanish conquistadors, lured by rumors of more treasures to the north, traveled into the present-day United States, including parts of Louisiana. In 1540, Francisco Vásquez de Coronado marched eastward from the Gulf of California to the Texas panhandle and Kansas. At the same time, Hernando de Soto traveled westward through the area north of what is now the Gulf of Mexico and reached the Mississippi River near Memphis, Tennessee. He crossed the river and wintered in Arkansas before turning back. The explorers were not interested in setting up colonies. Theirs was a quest for gold.

Hernando de Soto reaches the Mississippi River.

Later, Spanish missionaries and settlers arrived and set up towns and missions along the Gulf Coast and in the Southwest. The Spanish empire was the envy of Europe. France and England, however, were about to begin their voyages of discovery and expansion.

New France

France's presence in North America had humble beginnings. In the early 1500s, French fishermen arrived off the coast of present-day Nova Scotia, Canada. Cod was so abundant that the fishermen returned year after year.

As the men moved into what would be named the Gulf of Saint Lawrence, they met tribes of American Indians. The Indians' canoes were filled with animal furs. The Frenchmen, seeing a golden opportunity, traded axes, iron pots, or wool blankets for all the furs the Indians could acquire. By the 1630s, furs regularly left the upper Atlantic coast for Europe. The fur trade eventually brought wealth to France in the same way gold and silver did for Spain.

French settlement began in earnest in 1608 when Samuel de Champlain established the first trading post in Quebec. Champlain, known as the Father of New France, led expeditions up the Saint Lawrence River valley, getting as far as Lakes Huron and Ontario. The trading posts he set up eventually became permanent French settlements.

Throughout the seventeenth century, French explorers journeyed farther into the interior. For example, Jacques Mar-

The American Indian Pony

The Spaniards brought horses to the Americas. American Indians quickly recognized the swift-footed animals' potential. Horses became their wealth, their pride, and just what they needed to hunt buffalo.

quette and Louis Joliet traveled by canoe down the Mississippi until they reached the mouth of the Arkansas River. The explorations, settlements, and prosperous fur trade secured France's presence in North America.

Sieur de La Salle

Marquette and Joliet, the first white men to explore the Mississippi River

Sixty years after Champlain, the French explorer René-Robert Cavelier, Sieur de La Salle settled in Montreal, where he built a trading post. La Salle befriended the Indians, learned their languages, and listened to their tales of a great river that flowed south to salt water. In December 1681, La Salle

decided to search for a route to the sea. Accompanied by twenty-three Frenchmen and thirty-one American Indians, La Salle headed for the Mississippi River.

After a grueling journey that demanded great courage, the party reached the mouth of the Mississippi on April 9, 1682. As La Salle planted the banner of France and raised a cross, he proclaimed: "This country of Louisiana . . . in the name of the most high, mighty, invincible and victorious Louis the Great, by Grace of God King of France." La Salle claimed the whole of the Mississippi River valley for France. Louis XIV, king of France, was not impressed, however, and he told La Salle that these discoveries were useless.

Jean-Baptiste Le Moyne oversees the beginning of the building of New Orleans.

France Moves South

Within ten years, the king had a change of heart when he learned the Spaniards had established missions and forts along the Gulf Coast. With the king's blessing, French settlers began moving to Biloxi, in present-day Mississippi. The French explorer Jean-Baptiste Le Moyne, founded the port city of New Orleans in 1718. From then on, New Orleans would be the center of ship traffic on the Mississippi River that passed in and out of the Gulf of Mexico.

Other settlers, farmers, and a few fur traders set up outposts along the Mississippi and east into Illinois Territory. The settlements strengthened the link between the French colonies along the Saint Lawrence River and the Gulf Coast. Some Frenchmen hoped that in time, the Great Lakes region and the lower Mississippi would be joined into one grand French colony called La Nouvelle France, or New France.

New France was not to be, however. The French colony in North America remained a string of sparsely settled, far-flung trading posts and communities.

British Colonists

In contrast to the French, the English were primarily interested in land and settlements. Their colonies grew and prospered. A thriving economy developed from trade and production.

Population

As the eighteenth century began, fewer than 15,000 French settlers lived in North America, mostly in the Great Lakes region. In contrast, there were 350,000 English colonists living along the Atlantic seaboard.

The first permanent English settlement in North America was founded at Jamestown, Virginia, in 1607.

The French and Indian War was fought for control of the American continent.

English colonists eyed the green meadows, black soil, and thick forests of the land west of the Appalachian Mountains. Fur traders and land **speculators** pushed deep into what would become Kentucky and Ohio. Their frequent clashes and raids on French forts threatened France's claim on the land east of the Mississippi River.

French and Indian War

The disputes resulted in the French and Indian War (1754–1763), during which France fought England for control of the continent. With England's victory, France lost half its possessions in North America. The Treaty of Paris, signed in 1763, gave Canada and the French territory east of the Mississippi River to England. France retained New Orleans, the Louisiana Territory west of the Mississippi, and its rich sugarcane islands in the West Indies. Spain, which aided France in the conflict, lost East Florida and West Florida to England.

As a result, England controlled all of eastern North America. The Mississippi River became the boundary between the English, French, and Spanish empires. But in a secret agreement made the year before, France had already made changes to the boundary.

At that time, France considered the unmapped wilderness of the Louisiana Territory almost valueless in comparison to its rich and profitable island colony, Saint Domingue, in the Caribbean. So King Louis XV gave Louisiana to his cousin, King Charles III of Spain. Louis called it a reward for Spain's help in fighting the British forces. France no longer owned land on the continent. It was a bitter blow for many French people, who had dreamed of a French empire in North America.

Louis XV, king of France from 1715 to 1774

New Orleans

One of the most distinctive cities in North America began on mosquito-infested swamps, 110 miles (177 km) from the Gulf of Mexico. The town's founder, Sieur de Bienville, imagined a thriving city and port at the site where the deep Mississippi River runs strongly. He named the town Nouvelle Orléans (New Orleans) in honor of Duc d'Orléans, **regent** of France.

French, German, and other European settlers moved to the new town, and it grew slowly. In the mid-1700s, French Acadians left their homes and farms in Nova Scotia. Many moved to Louisiana, and they became known as Cajuns. The blending of many diverse cultures, languages, and traditions created a vibrant and unique city.

Don Antonio de Ulloa, the first Spanish governor of New Orleans

Chapter Three

Louisiana Under Spain

After France transferred Louisiana to Spain, it took four years before the first Spanish governor, Don Antonio de Ulloa, arrived in New Orleans. The French-speaking Creoles rebelled and forced de Ulloa to flee. A later governor, Don Luis de Unzaga, developed good relations with the citizens, and Spain governed the colony for the next thirty-four years.

England threatened Spanish Louisiana by setting up ports along the gulf,

Bernardo de Gálvez

building forts, and farming the land on the east side of the Mississippi. England wanted to control the traffic and trade on the river. And by the late eighteenth century, Spain was too weak and powerless to stop it.

Boundaries Change

But Spain found a way to strike back. In 1779, it declared war on England and helped the colonists in the American Revolution. The Spanish governor of Louisiana, Bernardo de Gálvez, gathered a small army of volunteers and Indians and defeated the British **garrisons** on the Mississippi River. England then surrendered its forts in West Florida. By war's end, boundaries east of the Mississippi shifted once more.

The Peace Treaty of 1783 ended the American Revolution. England retained Canada beyond Lake Superior but returned East Florida and West Florida to Spain. The United States gained the territory east of the Mississippi, south of Canada to Florida. Americans viewed the middle of the river as the boundary between Spanish Louisiana and the United States. King Charles III of Spain objected to the treaty. He wanted the area south of the Ohio River to be included with Spanish Louisiana.

Frontier Settlers

The Treaty of Paris guaranteed America's future, which included the right to expand westward. Americans headed westward in droves to claim land beyond the Appalachian Mountains. They often followed the **Wilderness Road,** which adventurer Daniel Boone marked off and cleared. Once the settlers reached a new territory, they cut down trees, cleared and plowed the soil, grew crops, and raised hogs and cattle. Trappers and hunters sought the abundant animals in the unspoiled forests for furs to use and trade.

Many farmers and fur trappers sought ways to send their goods to cities on the East Coast and in Europe, but the mountains stood as a barrier. Even with pack mules, the journey was long and difficult. The settlers had no choice but to turn to the rivers to get their products to markets.

Loaded onto **flatboats,** the furs, tobacco leaves, cured meats, and whiskey moved down the Ohio and Mississippi rivers to New Orleans. From there, the goods were shipped to ports around the world, where they were sold. But once the flatboats entered the waters of the lower Mississippi and New Orleans, they fell under the control of Spain.

A Growing Frontier

Settlers quickly filled the western frontier lands. By 1792, Kentucky had 221,000 settlers. It entered the Union as the fifteenth state on June 1 of that year. Tennessee followed on June 1, 1796, and Ohio on March 1, 1803.

Spain Breaks Treaty

Spain wanted to control not only the traffic on the Mississippi, but also the migration of Americans who were moving into Spanish territory. By placing military posts at Natchez and Vicksburg, in present-day Mississippi, Spain had prevented

England from giving up the east bank of the Mississippi River to the United States after the war. This resulted in Spain controlling both banks of the river.

Spanish officials often closed the Mississippi to American shippers, or they imposed a **duty** on their goods. In 1784, Count Floridablanca started river patrols and withdrew Americans' right to store goods. That action was in direct violation of the 1783 Treaty of Paris, which promised Americans the right to navigate the river and the right of deposit.

Western settlers reacted sharply. Spain's actions and the lack of support from the U.S. government frustrated them. Some settlers considered becoming Spanish citizens. Others demanded that the United States send troops and take command of the Mississippi River and New Orleans.

Many plotted to secede from, or leave, the Union and form a separate nation. General James Wilkinson of Kentucky became their leader. He **conspired** with Spain to control the Mississippi and to encourage Americans to switch loyalty from the United States to Spain.

United States leaders, however, had little time to think about Louisiana. They were busy drafting the Constitution.

Count Floridablanca

By 1789, Floridablanca had reason to reconsider his policies. He worried about reactions from the United States and England. Floridablanca ordered the river open again to Americans, subject to a 15 percent tax on goods. He also allowed Americans to immigrate to Louisiana if they took a loyalty oath to Spain. In exchange, the settlers received land grants and all commercial rights on the Mississippi.

In the next decade, change swept through Europe. And the United States began to grow as a nation.

Double Agent Number Thirteen

James Wilkinson, a soldier, trader, and, by all accounts, a **scoundrel,** served in the Revolutionary War (1775–1783). Afterward, he moved west with his family to Kentucky and became a merchant and trader.

In 1787, Wilkinson traveled to New Orleans and met with Spanish officials. They appointed him to represent them in Kentucky in exchange for a loan of $7,000. Wilkinson promised to promote the separation of western settlements in Kentucky and to bring them under Spanish rule.

To hide his spying activities from the U.S. government, Wilkinson wrote in code to the Spaniards. He became known as Secret Agent Number Thirteen.

In 1806, Wilkinson joined former vice president Aaron Burr and others in a secret plot to make Louisiana an independent republic. Wilkinson betrayed Burr by writing to President Jefferson, describing "the deep, dark, and widespread conspiracy." Burr was tried for treason, but found not guilty. Wilkinson also came under investigation, but he managed to conceal his role as a double agent. In fact, he was given command of New Orleans and received a promotion to the rank of major general in 1813.

George Washington faced many challenges as he led the United States through its first eight years.

Chapter Four

Struggling to Remain Neutral

With seven years of war behind them and the Constitution ratified, the House of Representatives elected George Washington as the nation's first president in 1789. Washington—a soldier and farmer—headed a new government that was plagued by financial problems, growing discontent in the West, and troubling foreign powers. It would take

The French Revolution began when French citizens stormed the Bastille, a prison, in 1789.

all his leadership skills, character, and prestige to steer the nation on a smooth course.

Washington turned to his gifted secretary of the treasury, Alexander Hamilton, to propose ways to pay off the large debt acquired during the American Revolution. Washington's greatest concerns, however, were the wars taking place in Europe. He thought it best to keep the United States neutral and not form any binding **alliances.**

The French Revolution

By the late 1700s, great dissatisfaction had swept through France. The discontent affected the peasants, middle-class merchants, and even the nobility. In 1789, the French Revolution began, and it lasted for a decade. The king was overthrown, and in 1792 the First French Republic replaced the monarchy.

But Citizen Genêt quickly stirred up trouble with his plans and schemes. He brought ships into Delaware Bay, an inlet of the Atlantic Ocean between New Jersey and Delaware, and manned them with pro-French Americans. He planned to capture British and Spanish merchant vessels.

Genêt also carried 250 French military **commissions.** They were to be used to recruit Americans for an army of liberation. The volunteer army would liberate Louisiana from Spain, and Canada from England. Then La Salle's dream of a French colony in North America would become a reality. To pay for his schemes, Genêt asked the U.S. Treasury to pay off some of its debt to France. Alexander Hamilton refused.

President Washington ordered Genêt to stop acting illegally. Washington feared that Genêt might involve the United States in France's war with England. Washington asked the

Edmond C. Genêt

French government to call Genêt home to France. The government agreed, because Genêt had not only angered Washington, but also had failed to deliver needed war supplies to France.

Jay's Treaty

After rejecting French demands for support, Washington sent representatives to England and Spain to improve relations and to resolve disputes with those nations.

Washington named Supreme Court chief justice John Jay as a special envoy to England. Jay spent months working out the terms of an agreement, later called Jay's Treaty. It was signed in November 1794. In the treaty, Britain agreed to remove its troops from the northwestern frontier by June 1796. It was England's final acceptance of America's right, by the earlier treaty, to the land east of the Mississippi.

In addition, Jay's Treaty allowed British citizens to collect debts owed to them from before the American Revolution. Britain, in turn, agreed to pay money for the illegal seizure of American ships. The treaty also declared the Mississippi River open to both countries.

Pinckney's Treaty

President Washington knew that he needed a similar treaty with Spain. Americans disputed the boundaries between Spanish Louisiana and the United States. They also opposed the closing of the Mississippi River and the port of New Orleans to American shipping.

Spanish officials in Louisiana, on the other hand, felt threatened by the number of American settlers moving west. Louisiana governor Barón de Carondelet wrote in his military report in 1794, "Their methods of spreading themselves and their policy are so much to be feared by Spain as are their arms."

Spain also had a new worry: France. Carondelet knew of Genêt's efforts to overthrow Spain in Louisiana. He thought Genêt had failed for lack of money, not support.

The United States and Spain agreed to renew negotiations. Washington sent Thomas Pinckney to Spain as the U.S. gov-

Piracy on the High Seas

Between 1793 and 1794, the British navy captured many American commercial ships headed for French ports. The English stole the goods and forced American sailors to serve in the British navy.

A flatboat hauls cargo down the Mississippi River.

ernment representative. Pinckney's patience and skill as a negotiator brought favorable results for the United States.

Spain recognized the 31st Parallel as the southern boundary of the United States. That expanded the U.S. border to what is now Natchez, Mississippi. The treaty granted free use of the Mississippi River to Americans for three years and the right to store their goods in New Orleans, free of tax. Spain agreed to renew these privileges if it was in that country's best interests.

Americans, and especially westerners, cheered Pinckney's Treaty. The new boundary unlocked more land for western pioneers. And the great Mississippi River would remain open to American shipping.

The Quasi War

France was alarmed by both treaties. French leaders believed the agreements strengthened the positions of England and Spain in North America. France responded to the perceived threats by acting aggressively toward the United States. The French navy captured American ships and sailors as ferociously as England had.

President John Adams and Vice President Thomas Jefferson both believed the attacks amounted to a quasi, or undeclared, war against the United States. Neither, however, desired to go to war with France, America's ally in the Revolution. Instead, President Adams sought a peaceful solution. He sent three ambassadors—one of them was Thomas Pinckney—to Paris to talk directly with Charles-Maurice de Talleyrand, the minister of foreign affairs.

Talleyrand stalled. Then he sent three agents to represent him. The agents demanded a loan to France from the United States and a large bribe to Talleyrand to end the maritime hostilities. Outraged, Pinckney said, "It is no! No! Not a **sixpence.**"

Americans marched in the streets, condemned France, and volunteered to defend the United States in war against France. Embarrassed, the French government asked President Adams to send new envoys to negotiate a peaceful settlement. The resulting Convention of 1800 restored diplomatic relations between France and the United States. But the harmony between the two nations would be tested in the coming years.

The Bishop of Autun

Educated as a priest, appointed a bishop, and elected to the French Parliament, Charles-Maurice de Talleyrand later served as a diplomat and statesman through several French regimes.

This famous painting shows Napoléon on horseback leading his troops into battle.

Chapter Five

Napoléon's Secret

As the nineteenth century began, a new leader emerged in France. Napoléon Bonaparte was a brilliant young army officer whose successful military campaigns attracted everyone's attention. As Napoléon's victories grew on the battlefield, so did his popularity, and he rose quickly to the rank of brigadier general.

Napoléon was an ambitious man. He had a vision of greatness for himself and France. In a bold move, he and his followers overthrew the French government and seized power in November 1799. Napoléon set up a three-member consulate and named himself first consul. From then on, he ruled as dictator of France.

A Secret Treaty

The French people had never abandoned their dreams of a colonial empire in North America. Many in the government believed that if France could regain Louisiana, it would be powerful enough to stop American expansion and prevent an alliance between England and the United States.

Napoléon thought he had found a way by negotiating a secret treaty with King Charles IV and Queen Maria Luisa of Spain in 1800. The king and queen agreed to exchange all of Spanish Louisiana for a small region of land in Italy. The royal couple wanted the land in Tuscany, with its art and culture, as a kingdom for their daughter.

The Spanish government was tired of supporting a territory that cost more than it earned. As a result, the Spaniards

Napoléon (standing at table) declares himself first consul of France.

thought they had gotten the better part of the deal. They reasoned that with France in Louisiana, England and the United States would be confined to their current boundaries. Spain then would be better able to protect its other immense land holdings in North America.

Napoléon promised Spain he would not sell or give away any portion of Louisiana to another country. Since he did not plan to take immediate possession of Louisiana, Napoléon insisted on secrecy. He feared that the Americans might attack the weak Spanish garrisons and take control of New Orleans.

King Charles IV (left) and Queen Maria Luisa (second from right), with their children and other family members

Saint Domingue

Before Napoléon could send troops to take possession of Louisiana, he wanted to return French rule to Saint Domingue, today known as the countries of Haiti and the Dominican Republic. The dictator saw the island as an important gathering area for his ships and troops heading for the North American continent. To control the island, Napoléon had to oust Toussaint-Louverture, the former slave who had become the governor-general of the island.

Jefferson Becomes President

While Napoléon dreamed of rebuilding France's former colony in America, Thomas Jefferson took office as the nation's third president.

Jefferson believed strongly in the freedom of the individual. He was confident that the future of the republic rested with everyday Americans, "the chosen people of God." He imagined a nation of farmers who, by working small plots of land, could transform the worthless wilderness into productive farmland.

Jefferson believed as George Washington did: The United States should remain neutral and not become involved in the affairs of other countries. However, Jefferson's attention, and that of his cabinet, centered on Napoléon's plans.

African slaves on Saint Domingue rebelled in 1791.

Carver's Story

A native of Massachusetts, **surveyor** Jonathan Carver wrote one of the first books about the land west of the Mississippi. Titled *Travels through the Interior Parts of North America in the Years 1766, 1767, 1768,* Carver's book gave a lively description of his explorations. He mapped the major rivers and determined the continent was 3,000 miles (4,800 km) wide. The book reached Jefferson and added to his interest about America's western lands.

Jonathan Carver

Despite Napoléon's request for secrecy, rumors spread that Spain had transferred Louisiana to France. In the spring of 1802, Jefferson learned that the rumors were true: France planned to take control of New Orleans and Louisiana.

Jefferson was certain that as long as another nation occupied New Orleans, the rights to navigate and store goods would be threatened. He expressed those thoughts when he wrote to Robert Livingston, the American representative in Paris: "The day that France takes possession of New Orleans fixes the sentence. . . . From that moment on, we must marry ourselves to the British fleet and nation." The possibility of the French army at America's border was unthinkable.

Defeat in Saint Domingue

Along with the news about Louisiana came word that thirty thousand French soldiers had arrived in Saint Domingue. Headed by Napoléon's brother-in-law, General Charles Leclerc, the French army planned to conquer the island, jail Toussaint-Louverture, and restore slavery.

But the troops were unprepared for the fierce resistance of Toussaint-Louverture's followers. Six months later, four-fifths of Leclerc's soldiers had died, either in battle or from yellow fever. Leclerc died of the disease, as well. Napoléon sent twenty thousand replacements with General Rochambeau. However, Rochambeau surrendered the following year. Napoléon's faith in a colonial empire in North America began to falter.

The Birth of Haiti

With the defeat of France, Toussaint-Louverture declared Saint Domingue an independent country, called Haiti.

Thomas Jefferson, the
third president of the
United States

Chapter Six

A Surprising Offer

Unexpectedly, Jefferson faced a new challenge. Spain canceled the Americans' right to store goods in New Orleans. Western farmers and merchants, as well as some Easterners, pressed Jefferson to take the city by force. The president massed a **militia** along the Mississippi frontier. He also decided to strengthen negotiations in Paris by appointing James Monroe to assist Robert Livingston.

Robert Livingston

Livingston had been trying for months to strike a deal for New Orleans, but had gotten nowhere. In a letter dated April 18, 1802, Jefferson wrote to Livingston: "There is on the globe one single spot, the possessor of which is our natural and habitual enemy. It is New Orleans, through which the produce of three-eighths of our territory must pass to market. . . . Every eye in the United States is now fixed on this affair of Louisiana."

A Shattered Dream

Some historians believe Napoléon lost interest in Louisiana after Leclerc's death, and decided that his future rested in Europe, not North America. The loss of thirty thousand French soldiers in Saint Domingue was crucial to his decision. Realistically, he did not have enough troops, money, or supplies to occupy both the island and Louisiana.

Other historians speculate that Napoléon wanted to invade Egypt, and to do so, he would have needed control of Malta, a group of islands in the Mediterranean Sea, south of Sicily.

Malta was controlled by England, which meant that Napoléon would have to declare war on that country.

In addition, Napoléon knew that Americans had openly expressed opposition to the French possession of Louisiana. He hoped to keep the United States neutral and on friendly terms with France, so Napoléon decided to sell Louisiana.

It is rumored that Napoléon confided to a friend, "I will not keep a possession . . . that may perhaps **embroil** me with the Americans, or may place me in a state of coolness with them. . . . My resolution is fixed; I will give Louisiana to the United States. . . . I shall demand a sum of money to pay the expenses of the extraordinary **armament** I am projecting against Great Britain."

France had learned—as Spain already knew—that American expansion westward could not be stopped. Napoléon's dream, and that of the French people, of La Nouvelle France was hopelessly shattered.

Take It All

"Let them give you one hundred million francs," Napoléon said to Francois de Barbé-Marbois, the minister of finance. "It is a lot of money to ask of a young country," Barbé-Marbois replied. Nevertheless, Barbé-Marbois relayed the offer to Livingston.

Meanwhile, Napoléon argued with his brothers about the sale. "Give this affair up as lost, both of you; you Lucien, on account of the sale in itself; you Joseph, because I shall get along without the consent of anyone whomsoever, do you understand?"

On April 15, 1803, Livingston and Monroe met with Barbé-Marbois. They began the bargaining with a counteroffer of forty million francs. It was not well received. Days of bargaining followed. On April 30, Livingston and Monroe accepted the price of sixty million francs, or fifteen million dollars.

"We have lived long, but this is the noblest work of our whole lives," Livingston said. "The treaty, which we have just signed has not been obtained by art or dictated by force; . . . it will change vast solitudes into flourishing districts. From this day the United States take their place among the powers of first rank."

Constitutional Dilemma

President Jefferson was elated by the news. It had always been his long-range plan to include the territory west of the Mississippi with the United States. But there was a problem. The Constitution had no provisions for obtaining new land or giving citizenship to people living outside the United States.

The situation greatly troubled Jefferson, who knew that it would take too much time to amend the Constitution. Jefferson put his misgivings aside and sent the treaty to Congress. Congress ratified the treaty on October 20, 1803, by a vote of twenty-four to seven.

An Abundant Land

In truth, no one knew what the United States had purchased, or what it meant for the country's future. Everyone knew, however, the United States now controlled boat traffic on the Mississippi River. Western settlers and traders in the Ohio Territory and Kentucky had safe passage for their goods through the port of New Orleans.

Within decades, Americans would learn that the region held rich mineral resources such as oil, coal, and iron. There

Western lands were quickly settled following the Louisiana Purchase.

The Louisiana Purchase paved the path for homesteaders and pioneers who would settle on America's frontier.

were thick forests of tall pines, bald cypress, oaks, and cottonwoods. In many areas, long winding rivers and large lakes provided abundant freshwater and fish. The eastern side of the Louisiana Purchase consisted of good soil for farming. Farther west, the rolling grasslands held promise for grazing cattle.

By the 1850s, the young nation began to take shape, as a steady stream of pioneers crossed the Mississippi River and settled in the new land—and beyond. The waves of homesteaders continued for a hundred years until farms, towns, and cities could be found from the Atlantic to the Pacific.

Timeline

1500s	Spain sends explorers, such as de Soto and Coronado, into the Louisiana Territory in search of gold.
1682	La Salle claims Louisiana Territory for France. It extends east and west of the Mississippi River and reaches from Canada to the Gulf of Mexico.
1718	Sieur de Bienville establishes a colony in New Orleans and makes it the capital of the French colony of Louisiana.
1754– 1763	The French and Indian War results in France losing its possessions on the North American continent.
1762	In a secret treaty, the king of France turns over Louisiana and the port of New Orleans to Spain.
1766	The first Spanish governor arrives in New Orleans.
1775– 1783	In the American Revolutionary War, France and Spain aid the Americans. The Peace Treaty gives the United States the territory east of the Mississippi River from Canada to Florida.
1784	Spanish officials close the port of New Orleans to Americans.
1789	Spain reopens the river and port to Americans, subject to a 15 percent tax.
1791– 1801	Slaves rebel on Saint Domingue. Toussaint-Louverture, a former slave, leads the rebellion and becomes governor-general.

1794	England signs Jay's Treaty and agrees to evacuate the northwestern forts by 1796. In Pinckney's Treaty, Charles IV of Spain gives Americans free use of the Mississippi and the right to deposit goods in New Orleans for three years.
1799	Napoléon seizes power in France.
1800	In a secret treaty with Spain, Napoléon exchanges a small area in Italy for New Orleans and Louisiana west of the Mississippi.
1801	Thomas Jefferson becomes the third president of the United States.
1802	King Charles IV of Spain officially transfers Louisiana to France. Before the transfer, Spanish officials in New Orleans close the port to American shipping again. Jefferson instructs Robert Livingston, U.S. minister to France, to negotiate the purchase of New Orleans and East and West Florida.
1802–1803	French troops arrive on Saint Domingue to put down the rebellion and oust Toussaint-Louverture. France is defeated. Jefferson appoints James Monroe to assist Livingston with the negotiations for the Louisiana Purchase.
1803	Napoléon sells Louisiana to the United States. Congress ratifies the treaty on October 20.

Glossary

alliance—an agreement between two or more countries to work together

armament—military force

commissions—certificates of military rank that can be given to those who join the military

conspire—to join in a secret plan to perform an illegal act

Continental Divide—in North America, the area of land that runs south from northwestern Canada, along the Rocky Mountains, to New Mexico; east of the divide, water drains into the Atlantic Ocean, and west of the divide, water drains into the Pacific Ocean

duty—a tax on imported goods

embroil—to involve oneself or another in conflict or difficulty

flatboat—a boat with a flat bottom and square ends used for transporting goods in shallow water

franc—the basic unit of money used in France until 2002

garrison—a permanent military post

militia—a group of citizens who are trained to fight

musket—a gun with a long barrel that was used before the rifle was invented

negotiate—to bargain or discuss something in order to reach an agreement

prefect—a high-ranking official or government leader

regent—a ruler or governor

republic—a country with a form of government in which the people elect representatives to manage the government

scoundrel—someone who cheats and lies

sixpence—a coin equal to six pennies

speculator—a person who buys land and then sells it for a profit

surveyor—a person who measures an area of land in order to make a map

ultimatum—a final demand or proposition

Wilderness Road—the trail blazed through the Appalachian Mountains from Virginia to Kentucky that eastern settlers followed to reach the fertile lands of the West

windfall—a sudden piece of good news or good luck

To Find
Out More

Books

Blumberg, Rhoda. *What's the Deal? Jefferson, Napoleon and the Louisiana Purchase*. Washington, D.C.: National Geographic Society, 1998.

Collier, Christopher, and James Lincoln Collier. *The Jeffersonian Republicans: The Louisiana Purchase and the War of 1812*. Tarrytown, N.Y.: Benchmark Books, 1998.

Gaines, Ann Graham. *The Louisiana Purchase in American History*. Berkeley Heights, N.J.: Enslow, 2000.

Hakim, Joy. *The New Nation*. New York: Oxford University Press, 1993.

Lewis, James E., Jr. *The Louisiana Purchase: Jefferson's Noble Bargain?* Washington, D.C.: Thomas Jefferson Memorial Association, 2003.

Macaulay, Ellen. *Louisiana.* Danbury, Conn.: Children's Press, 2003.

Organizations and Online Sites

Encyclopedia Louisiana
http://enlou.com
This site includes letters and documents about Louisiana history.

Napoléon Bonaparte Internet Guide
http://www.napoleonbonaparte.nl/
This site provides links to information about Napoléon.

National Museum of American History
http://americanhistory.si.edu
This site is part of the Smithsonian Institution. This site contains a time line of American history and a site search where you can find more information about the Louisiana Purchase.

U.S. National Archives & Records Administration
www.archives.gov/
Here you can view the actual Louisiana Purchase treaty.

A Note on Sources

My research began at home and in the library, where I searched for as many history books as I could find. Standard references included Samuel Morison's *The Oxford History of the American People* and Marshall Sprague's *So Vast, So Beautiful a Land.* Alexander de Conde's *The Affair of Louisiana,* Martin Hintz's *Louisiana,* and David Colbert's *Eyewitness to America* proved very helpful.

Many books were biographies of Thomas Jefferson. Frank Irwin's *Letters of Thomas Jefferson* provided a primary reference that I used for quotations in the manuscript. I also looked through children's books to see the way in which the authors handled the subject.

Web sites, such as The White Oak Society and Encyclopedia Louisiana, offered additional biographical, historical, and factual information.

—*Gloria G. Schlaepfer*

Index

Numbers in *italics* indicate illustrations.

About the Author

A graduate of Douglass College, Rutgers University, and California State University-Fullerton, Gloria Schlaepfer earned a bachelor's degree in biology and a master's degree in environmental studies. Her master's thesis topic was an oral history of the preservation efforts to save an endangered species. Gloria is the coauthor of three nature books, including *Pythons and Boas*, published by Watts Library in 2002. She has also written two other books on animals. Schlaepfer lives in California with her husband, Karl, and has four children and four grandchildren.